Minute Motivators for the Military

*Quick Inspiration for the
Time of Your Life*

Stan Toler

and

Brig Gen (Ret.) Robert R. Redwine

BEACON HILL PRESS
OF KANSAS CITY

Contents

1. Leadership 6
2. Optimism 8
3. Correction 10
4. Motivation 12
5. Preparation 14
6. Perfection 16
7. Integrity 18
8. Bravery 20
9. Diplomacy 22
10. Determination 24
11. Confidence 26
12. Compassion 28
13. Patience 30
14. Originality 32
15. Honesty 34
16. Compromise 36
17. Duty 38
18. Authority 40
19. Decisiveness 42
20. Attitude 44
21. Perseverance 46
22. Effort 48
23. Grief 50
24. Discipline 52
25. Humility 54
26. Strength 56
27. Persistence 58
28. Ethic 60
29. Patriotism 62
30. Courtesy 64
31. Resolve 66
32. Purpose 68
33. Influence 70

34. Risk.....................................72
35. Adversity..............................74
36. Planning 76
37. Responsibility 78
38. Excellence.............................80
39. Discernment 82
40. Family.................................84
41. Recovery..............................86
42. Details.................................88
43. Audacity 90
44. Impact.................................92
45. Faith 94
46. Flexibility.............................96
47. Values.................................98
48. Readiness 100
49. Hope 102
50. Loyalty 104
51. Thought...............................106
52. Perspective 108
53. Opinion...............................110
54. Vision 112
55. Gossip 114
56. Procrastination 116
57. Diversity..............................118
58. Touch 120
59. Giving.................................122
60. Experience 124
61. Example 126
62. Honor 128
63. Presence 130
64. Healing 132
65. Ego 134
66. Ideals.................................136
67. Creativity 138
68. Attitude...............................140
69. Adversity..............................142
70. Worry 144
71. Humor.................................146

Chapter 1

Leadership

If you walk around undefeated—

so will they!

—General Stephen Lorenz

Every team needs a coach—a leader.

The rise or fall of any championship sports team rests largely on the shoulders of its coach. Obviously, the skills of its players are a critical link to a winning season as well, but skill without leadership is unproductive at best and catastrophic at worst.

There must be a leader capable of producing a game plan—a strategy—for forging those talents and capabilities into a strong, unified effort to maximize the team's potential. Just as importantly, championship teams reflect a coach's winning behavior and character through their performance and desire to win.

Similarly, military leaders understand they set the example for their teams. They understand that organizational climate—how individual members perceive their team and its capacity for success—is their job, their responsibility. They know their own actions and attitudes will inevitably be mirrored by those they lead.

So, they show confidence in themselves and others. They don't get too high following success or too low following a setback. They remain poised and calm. They remain tough and show strength, even smile, in the face of adversity. They refuse to entertain the thought of failure.

If you will lead a championship-caliber team, you will lead with your life—your example—not just with your orders. You will set the tone. You will model in person what you want your followers to demonstrate in practice.

Chapter 2

Optimism

We're surrounded . . . that simplifies

our problem.

—Lt. General Chesty Puller

Every cloud has a silver lining.

Seventeenth-century writer John Milton birthed the thought that has become one of the most well-known proverbs of modern times. It suggests that no matter how foreboding the clouds, there is a ray of brightness above them.

Great military leaders never stop believing in the win. They find the silver lining in the most difficult circumstances; it is built into their DNA. Ideas and solutions flow from that glimmer of promise shining in their soul. You might call it a "silver-lining syndrome."

Where does this optimism come from? It comes from remembering that one nameless warrior who first dared to dream of victory in the face of defeat and raised the first bloodied banner of hope over the battlefield of doubt. It comes from recalling past personal successes in overcoming challenges. It comes from confidence in the team's collective ability.

Remember your first airline flight on an overcast day? Remember how beautiful and bright the skies were once the plane broke through the clouds? Even seasoned travelers still feel drawn to the spectacular view from their aisle window. Perhaps it is a sign that we are all inspired by breaking through the clouds.

Maybe you are encountering a glass-half-empty environment. Perhaps you have experienced more partly cloudy days than partly sunny days in your personal life.

Make your own breakthrough; part your own clouds. Dare to be optimistic about a seemingly pessimistic situation. Even when you are surrounded by the enemy, raise the banner of hope and conquer the challenge with determination and optimism.

Chapter 3

Correction

You don't lead by hitting people over

the head—that's assault,

not leadership.

—General of the U.S. Army Dwight D. Eisenhower

It happens almost every day. Someone on a leader's watch fails an assignment. The failure causes a ripple effect: a schedule is missed, the timeline is disrupted, and the mission itself is threatened. Someone must be held accountable.

Truly effective leadership is not easy. Lessons must be taught with a positive outcome in view. Not only must the operation be salvaged, but so must the offender.

Military leaders must accomplish the mission and develop their people. There are unquestionably times where it is appropriate to instill a sense of urgency. However, angry words can't reverse time. Standing alone, irate words accomplish neither the mission nor the development of personnel.

Remember your own career failures? How were you treated, and what effect did it have on you? How were you motivated to face it and go on?

If you were fortunate, your superior was patient enough to recognize your potential, firm enough to make appropriate correction, and wise enough to use the experience to develop your strengths. That's called tough love, an interesting mix of plastic and steel—one showing flexibility, the other firmness.

Ultimately, your job is to salvage the salvageable. Ask yourself what you can do to enforce accountability yet minimize accusation. How might you enhance the future value of the offender to the service and your organization?

Review the assignment. Did it match the skill set of the individual? Were sufficient resources made available?

Consider your reaction. Was your correction constructive? Did you sandwich the negative with positives?

You can turn a bad situation into a great learning experience.

Chapter 4

Motivation

Motivation is the art of getting people

to do what you want them to do

because they want to do it.

—General of the U.S. Army Dwight D. Eisenhower

Courtesy, collegiality, and respect trump harshness any day of the week.

The reason is simple: in the end, military excellence is more a product of motivated and skilled people than it is high-tech weaponry. Developing positive interpersonal relationships and a sense of teamwork are critical. In many ways, military life and corporate life are similar in this regard. The success of a mission or a business endeavor rests on motivating leaders and staff to be and do their very best.

Merriam-Webster defines motivation as the act or process of giving someone a reason for doing something. From your earliest days, you have been on the receiving end of motivation. In fact, your whole life is built around it. In high school, getting good grades or competing in sports may have pushed you to excel. In college, career goals provided impetus. Now, the opportunity to serve your country with distinction and advance your individual career is an invisible thumb in your back.

Do you see the pattern? What motivated you, benefited you.

Military leaders who excel are those who can produce excellence through motivating their people. How? Never miss an opportunity to articulate how one person's job, or one unit's role, contributes to the overall success of the mission. Remind them they are part of something much larger than themselves. Explain the why—or rationale—behind your direction or request. Ask for input. Honor excellence. Take advantage of each opportunity to nominate deserving individuals or units for medals, commendations, or quarterly or annual awards. Remember birthdays. Visit the sick or wounded. Congratulate those with a newborn.

The things that motivate you are the same things that motivate others.

Chapter 5

Preparation

Untutored courage is useless in the

face of educated bullets.

—General George S. Patton

The Air Force NCO took aside a very enthusiastic young second lieutenant and whispered to him this advice: "Sir, just make sure you're not one of those guys that is all thrust and no vector."

The sergeant's meaning was clear. The enthusiasm was fine, but the young officer needed to think about his goal and plan to achieve an objective. In short, he needed to prepare in order to be successful.

Your personal life is a journey made up of past education, training, and experience, future plans and objectives, and present reality. Combine those factors with courageous vision and thorough preparation, and you will reach your destination. Leave one out, and you will grind to a halt or lose your way altogether. New York Yankee Yogi Berra put it this way, "If you don't know where you are going, you'll end up somewhere else."

The same ingredients necessary for personal success are vital to effective leadership as well. You plan your mission based on your experience, and you take steps according to learned skills in military science.

Taking action and seizing the initiative are always critical to military success. But taking action without preparation is a pipe dream at best and dangerous at worst. Every action has an underlying premise. Each task is driven by the intent to accomplish a specific objective. Preparation and training is how you get there. Your Creator placed within you a logic that commands actions to your brain, through your heart to your hand. So you train tirelessly—mastering the task through repetition until it becomes routine. Pray, plan, relentlessly prepare, train, and work until you are ready to face the worst situations with your very best, overcoming adversity to achieve victory.

Chapter 6

Perfection

Be the Best

—Master Chief Petty Officer Carl Brashear,
the first African-American diver in the U.S. Navy

Whoever was the first to say, "Nobody's perfect," said it perfectly.

Have you ever met persons with type A-plus personalities? Never mind bouncing a quarter off their bunk, they could bounce a feather. They rode torpedoes to make sure they hit the targets in just the right spot. Perhaps that is a bit exaggerated, but you get the picture.

Pity the persons like them—and pity the persons in their branch of the service who think they must be like them. Being absolutely perfect is about as much fun as wearing a jacket of porcupine quills. Their lives are a constant shuffling and re-shuffling, trying to put things in manageable rows or columns. If they haven't fallen over the obsessive-compulsive disorder cliff, they're tiptoeing on the edge.

"Be the best," Carl Brashear says to each of us. "Impossible!" we whisper under our breath. In our hearts we know that we can't even trust a WET PAINT sign without expressing our unbelief with a quick swipe.

Where can we land this aircraft without demolishing the tower? Let's think of perfection as more of a personal best than the best. Being the best is an effort on the move rather than a static condition.

Your best is the best you can do. It is your best effort. It is releasing your best ability to accomplish the assignment. It is overcoming obstacles. It is constantly seeking improvement. It is you, at your best.

Chapter 7

Integrity

The supreme quality for leadership is
unquestionably integrity. Without it,
no real success is possible.

—General of the U.S. Army Dwight D. Eisenhower

The ability to lead others is never more important than the ability to lead yourself.

When you realize that you are the captain of your character, you will have completed perhaps the most vital training of your life. Every decision must comply with your orders as established in your values code. And every action must spring from the well of your integrity.

Leaders lead; they set the mark of principles. They raise the bar of excellence, and their troops follow their orders for a while, but they follow their example for a lifetime.

Integrity isn't factory installed, however. It is manufactured daily on the assembly line of your attitudes and actions. You are both the line supervisor and the line worker, following the standards of a higher authority.

Every automobile is known by its VIN, its vehicle identification number. As you probably know, the letters and numbers identify the manufacturer and its country of origin, the model and engine type, and the date of origin. Each VIN is unique—and separates one auto from others in the manufacturing plant.

Just as the auto identification is stamped into the auto's frame, the integrity of your life's product is stamped on you. It will last beyond your lifetime, so you make sure that it reflects the quality of your work.

Chapter 8

Bravery

History does not long entrust the care

of freedom to the weak or timid.

—General of the U.S. Army Dwight D. Eisenhower

Inside the Pentagon's A-ring there is a stained-glass mural showing four lieutenants looking over a sinking ship. A similar mural is found in the Army War College chapel at Carlisle Barracks. These murals commemorate the actions of four U.S. Army chaplains on the night of February 3, 1943, the night a German U-boat torpedoed a U.S. Army transport ship—the USAT Dorchester.

Men scrambled on deck and began boarding lifeboats soon after the torpedo hit. Some of the lifeboats were damaged, however. The chaplains began distributing life vests, and then, when the supply ran out, they willingly gave up their own life vests to soldiers who were without. They comforted, prayed with, and ultimately died with those who could not leave the sinking ship. They were posthumously awarded the Distinguished Service Cross and later a specially enacted Congressional Medal for Heroism.

Bravery is the unseen armor of every soldier, sailor, airman, or marine. It is the stuff of conquerors and the building blocks of freedom and justice. Behind history's great military achievements are corporate or individual acts of courage, in spite of consequences; most are unknown or unspoken, and all beloved by its benefactors.

The brave aren't blind to the armament of the enemy or deaf to its threats. Nor are they oblivious to the risks and potential consequences. They have much to live for. Indeed, three of the four "immortal chaplains" had families—wives and children at home. The brave just act or react on trained impulse. They believe right will win over wrong, even at its highest cost.

How can you be braver? Realize that bravery doesn't rely on brawn. It uses the brain; it believes in a higher calling, it is optimistic. It leverages faith.

Learn that, and you will be a brave leader.

Chapter 9

Diplomacy

We need talented and thoughtful
leaders who have a deep and abiding
appreciation for other cultures,
languages, and customs.

—General Norton Schwartz

R-E-S-P-E-C-T is more than a lyric to an Aretha Franklin song. And it is more than a quick military salute to a senior officer in passing. Respect is a personal decision to recognize the individual worth and experience of another.

Respect is also a key trait for effective diplomacy. Many may not readily associate the word diplomacy with the military. However, insightful leaders recognize being diplomatic as a valuable tool for both occupational and leadership reasons.

FreeDictionary.com defines diplomacy as: (1) the art and practice of international relations and, (2) tact and skill in dealing with people.

- Diplomatic leaders show grace and tact.
- Diplomatic leaders acknowledge the views, abilities, and contributions of others.
- Diplomatic leaders disagree agreeably.
- Diplomatic leaders resolve misunderstandings in a constructive manner.
- Diplomatic leaders are polite.

We live in a modern era of globalization. The world is more tightly connected than ever before in terms of communication, transportation, and commerce. Globalization clearly impacts the profession of arms as well. The U.S. military is deployed and engaged throughout the world, and we work daily with host nations and international partners. Showing sensitivity to local norms and customs is particularly important in areas of conflict. As General Schwartz suggests, the most effective military leaders will prepare by learning about—and from—the international community.

Such leadership produces understanding; understanding, in turn, produces common ground; common ground produces success.

Chapter 10

Determination

It is fatal to enter a war without the

will to win it.

—General Douglas MacArthur

Olympic runner Glenn Cunningham was considered the greatest miler of all time. His legs were horribly burned in a school accident, and his physicians considered leg amputation. But he began a grueling rehabilitation that resulted in his relearning to walk, and two years later he began to run. Amazingly, Cunningham competed in the 1932 and 1936 Summer Olympics, winning a silver medal in the 1936 Games.

How do you face the day? Do you face it with a determination to win, or are you content with being a good loser? Determination is a 365-day-of-every-year possibility.

Determination is an attitude that must be developed. You may have been born into a household that fostered a loser mentality, where, subconsciously, getting by was more important than getting ahead. But you don't live there anymore. You've moved on. You've discovered a uniqueness that sets you apart. Bring it!

Once you have discovered your unique skill, train it; become more skillful. Be the best you can be. Of course, it will take personal sacrifice, but sacrifice is at the core of determination.

When you see the competition loom over you, resize it. You can do it. You are determined, and you can conquer this. Stretch your faith. What you believe in can help you overcome what you are concerned about. Start with the winner's trophy in your heart, and you will hold it in your hand later on.

Chapter 11

Confidence

Confidence doesn't come out of

nowhere. It's a result of something . . .

hours and days and weeks and years of

constant work and dedication.

—Roger Staubach,
National Football League quarterback, and Lieutenant, USN

Are you a gearhead? Does your collection of electronic gadgets give you a techie edge?

Imagine a world without circuit boards and apps. The devices we hold in our hands are always more powerful than their first generation. Whether it is the latest operating system or largest storage system, we are a culture of digital dominance.

Then, the dreaded blue screen appears. The latest download won't sync. Your day's work or play comes to a screeching halt; your attitude changes. Anger rises above your level of pride. Suddenly your precious piece of metal or plastic is nothing more than an ornament held or displayed to prove how trendy you are.

Certain military leadership traits are timeless. Confidence doesn't need technology. The leader can instill such a sense of confidence in his or her troops that they will refuse to consider, much less entertain, the thought of failure.

People may be drawn to what you have, but they stay because of who you are. Those who stay are in need of the confidence you exude. They crave it more than the next tablet or smartphone upgrade. Leading with confidence is a natural recruiter. People gravitate toward those who are success minded.

Don't be a techno-slave. The brain God installed in you is a thousand times more efficient than the latest digital gadget. You learn by observing and doing. Computers learn when you input what you have observed and learned. Case closed.

Chapter 12

Compassion

The day soldiers stop bringing you
their problems is the day you have
stopped leading them. They have
either lost confidence that you can help
or concluded you do not care. Either
case is a failure of leadership.

—General Colin Powell

Leaders are problem solvers by nature or nurture.

Some of history's greatest military leaders have been people of great compassion. Sure, they were tough when needed. Granted, they could issue a directive order with the language of authority when the situation required. But their love for their country and its defenders brought with it a spirit of compassion.

Face it; some in the military may still confuse demonstrating compassion with a lack of leadership firmness and strength. Yet, properly understood, strength and compassion are complementary military leadership traits. The truly effective leader understands that the challenges of leading this generation of soldiers, sailors, marines, and airmen require a leadership approach of inspiration and not intimidation. This is especially true during a protracted period of combat.

Do your fellow troops know you care about them? How do you show respect for their individual worth? Do you rebuke sparingly and never hesitate to offer praise for a job well done? Are you a good listener? Do you share advice without a know-it-all attitude?

Do you make eye-contact during your conversation? Do you have a strict code of keeping personal information confidential? Do you share grief and joys with the same enthusiasm?

Positive answers to these questions indicate the character quality of compassion. Congratulations! You have the qualities of compassionate leadership. And you have a firm grasp on the Golden Rule—doing unto others what you would want done to you.

Chapter 13

Patience

Get mad, then get over it.

—General Colin Powell

Your patience will be sorely tried in the military.

This comes as no surprise to those who have served. Indeed, initial military training brings with it an early introduction to the military's unique brand of hurry-up-and-wait. Hustling only to reach another very long, very slow-moving line can certainly try one's patience, but compared to other situations, it ranks pretty low on the patience scale. Working with people with difficult personalities is probably near the top—and almost everyone has met a few chart busters in his or her career.

It's too bad that patience isn't issued along with dog tags. Both will be needed at some time or another, and both can be used to identify you.

Impatience is a first cousin to anger, and each can be used for good or evil. Anger can be used positively for personal, familial, or unit protection. Used at the wrong time or for the wrong purpose, though, and it can mean a heap of trouble. Impatience has a good side as well. It keeps people from parking in the status-quo lot. It motivates spiritual, physical, social, financial, and career excellence.

Appropriate patience isn't purchased on eBay; it is acquired. You can start by recognizing that many irritants are simply unworthy of a response. In other words, learn what to ignore or overlook. You can discipline yourself to work on the most critical task at hand while you wait for other factors to align themselves. A naval aviator's admonition, "don't lunge for the ball," is a good figurative illustration for this advice.

Patience also takes practice. Thomas Jefferson once said, "When angry, count to ten before you speak; when very angry, count to a hundred." Whether you do the counting thing or take a walk when you face an explosive situation, you are practicing your patience. It also has an eventual reward, complete with greater respect, recognition, authority, and responsibility.

Chapter 14

Originality

If everyone is thinking alike, then

somebody isn't thinking.

—General George S. Patton

The classic bumper sticker quote says, "You're an original — just like everyone else."

That may draw attention, but it isn't factual. You are an original, from the retinas of your eyes to the prints of your palms. Other people may have the ability to lead, but none will lead like you. You bring a personal uniqueness to the military.

You have a unique outlook. Some see forests, others see trees. Your eye is sharpened for what could be. Others discern what should have been. Both offer solutions based on their outlook.

You have unique talents. Others have their own unique strengths. Imagine a band that has only drums. Its concerts not only would be boring but also would border on annoying. Bands require a variety of instruments in the hands of instrumentalists who have a unique method and sound. Blended together, the variety is played out in spectacular fashion. You might be a broad-stroke leader who can envision and organize a project for completion. Others are fine-stroke leaders who excel in seeing an organized project through to completion.

You have unique people skills. Your unique life experiences blend with your unique personality to fit socially with other people. For example, if everyone was the life of the party, it would be a chaotic scene. Some excel at telling jokes or stories, while others listen — and are probably the better for it.

As a leader, it is important to recognize that each individual has his or her own unique strengths. To gain the maximum benefit from each of those strengths, you must make sure people feel comfortable speaking up and providing you with their perspective, their views — including ones at odds with your own.

Celebrate who you and each of your troops are: an original.

Chapter 15

Honesty

I hope I shall possess firmness and
virtue enough to maintain what I
consider the most enviable of all titles,
the character of an honest man.

—General George Washington

General Washington set the expectation: honesty is clearly the standard in the military. It is a foundational trait upon which loyalty, trust, and confidence are built. Outright lying is rarely the issue in today's military for the simple reason that lying and mendacity are not tolerated. However, there are aspects of honesty, beyond simple truthfulness, that warrant special attention in the military environment.

Honesty includes strict adherence to fact; in other words, being intellectually honest. Possess the firmness to avoid group-think. Resist the pressure to reach a conclusion or take a position that is simply not supported by the facts. Be willing to tell the boss bad news. Be willing, tactfully and appropriately, to tell the boss when he or she is wrong or mistaken. Be willing to discuss the elephant-in-the-room issue that no one else will raise.

Honesty also includes the concept of straightforwardness—of candidness. Some, in an effort to play it safe and avoid being wrong, will offer advice that is so general it does not really say anything. If you're asked what you think, then say what you think. Explain your rationale. It is far better to provide clear and specific views and occasionally be wrong than it is to develop an overly cautious reputation as one who uses a great deal of words but says nothing of value.

Some mistakenly take candidness a step too far. They pride themselves in being brutally honest. But nothing about honesty requires that views be delivered in an arrogant or surly manner. In the end, doing so is counterproductive.

Provide intellectually honest, straightforward views. Others will seek your perspective, and you will increase your value to your boss and your organization.

Chapter 16

Compromise

Being right is necessary—

but it is not sufficient.

—Air Force General Raymond Johns

Compromise has a bad reputation. It is often wrongly perceived as the undesired result of one side or the other caving on important principles. But compromise for the sake of a right cause is a practical option that can also achieve valuable cohesion. Indeed, the United States Constitution, which military members are sworn to defend, was itself a product of compromise for the sake of achieving unity around a worthy cause.

Compromise has its place in the military as well. Differences can and do occur between individuals, units, organizations, and services. Regardless of rank, in order to be truly effective, you must learn to persuade, negotiate, build consensus, and build relationships, especially with key stakeholders. Sometimes this means compromise and understanding the art of the deal—as well as its long-term benefits. To use a football analogy, sometimes you can't complete the long ball for a quick touchdown; you just have to get a first down and move the chains closer to the goal line.

You can proclaim yourself right on a matter for all the wrong reasons. For example, you may think your position is being threatened. Or you may perceive the actions of another have crossed the property line of your authority area. So with teeth grinding and fists clenching, you stand your ground—even if it's shaky ground. You may insist on all or nothing—and achieve nothing.

Evaluate your idea. Is it right? If so, ask yourself whether this is the right time to advance your idea and whether you have coordinated it in a transparent manner with all others who have equities in the issue. At all costs, avoid becoming hostile or moody when others don't see the issue the same way you do, even if you are right. Relax. Look for common ground, and then look for a way that positives from both sides can reach a common agreement. You may have to go farther than half way, but the destination is worth the journey.

Chapter 17

Duty

Any soldier worth his salt should be
antiwar. And still there are things
worth fighting for.

—General Norman Schwarzkopf

It's a tough job, but somebody has to do it.

That phrase is usually the caption to a luxurious setting. Sun-tanned tourists search the horizon of white, sandy beach, while foam-crested waves play tag with their toes before making a hasty retreat.

Military personnel see it from a different angle. Often their assignment is a sea change from an idyllic beach setting. They may search the horizon, but they're not thinking about sunsets or sunrises or the composition of the beach sand. They think about home—about the thousands of miles that often separate them from the ones they love.

They know that the quiet of a night can be broken by the crackle of gunfire and the cries of the wounded. They have their moments when they would rather be anywhere other than where they are, but they will not leave. They are where they are because of their sense of duty.

And duty keeps them there despite the difficult living conditions, the exceptionally long days, the danger, and the family separation.

You had no idea how many times you would be required to dig down deep to draw your sense of duty to the surface, but you did—and still do. You know too much is at stake for you to abandon the post that your eternally grateful country asked you to guard.

Chapter 18

Authority

Those who enjoy responsibility

usually get it; those who merely like

exercising authority usually lose it.

—Malcolm Forbes,
publisher and former staff sergeant, U.S. Army

Like an episode of TV's "Survivor Island," when you put a group of people together, someone will eventually take charge.

Leaders may be given a rank at graduation, but true authority is earned on the job. Authority comes from the inside. It agonizes over a mission's leadership gap and yearns to help solve the problem. It is confident its answers are right—even if they are later proven wrong.

Its motto is "Take charge!"

Obviously, authority can be abused. The roving eyes of social media prove it on an almost daily basis. Its abuses go viral, and abusers are eternally shamed in the archives of the Internet.

But authority can also be used positively.

Rightful authority is prepared. It goes to school on the experience of others. For example, what person of authority most influenced you, and why? You will spot some characteristics that can be mirrored in your own life.

- What was that person's attitude? If it was condescending, it probably failed.
- How were that person's orders given? If they were unclear, they were probably misleading.
- Was that person's correction practical and helpful? If not, it was probably forgotten.
- Were you given affirmation from that person? If not, they were probably self-serving.

Authority that abuses results is authority that is refused. You will know the difference before, during, and after that incident that defined your leadership. As a leader, you can give meaningful and effective orders, but orders that don't reflect a basic respect for another are simply over-exercised futilities.

Chapter 19

Decisiveness

It is better to do the wrong thing,

than to do nothing.

—Prime Minister Winston Churchill

The sergeant listened to the recruit explain his rationale for failing to move out promptly during a small unit training exercise. He then said, "Son, the purpose of this exercise is to show me that you can make a quick decision under duress. We'll worry later about whether you are actually making the right decisions."

Decisiveness, the ability to make quick and confident decisions, is indeed a critical military leadership trait.

Acting decisively is not an invitation to act rashly. Rashness is acting without thought about what will happen as a result of a decision. Rather, the decisive military leader does not overthink or overanalyze a situation.

Decisiveness begins by identifying and giving priority to those issues that require timely decision. Not all require immediate attention. Some do warrant more careful study or analysis. Even in those circumstances, the decisive leader will not hesitate to make a decision when sufficient data is available.

Other decisions, especially ones involving battle, require an immediate call. In those circumstances, first recognize, as Sir Winston Churchill suggests, that doing nothing is itself a decision and frequently it is the worst decision of all. Second, understand that it is highly unlikely that you will ever have perfect information. Learn to trust your instincts and rely on your experience. Make the call. Take action.

Chapter 20

Attitude

I think, whether you're having
setbacks or not, the role of a leader is
to always display a winning attitude.

—General Colin Powell

A ttitudes are more often caught than taught.

The old adage says it all. Every soldier, sailor, airman, or marine has an attitude—negative, positive, or both, and those attitudes frequently correlate directly to the attitude of leadership.

Lead with sullenness or arrogance, and the response of individuals and your organization are predictably negative. Their performance will prove disappointing as well. Lead with a positive, winning attitude, and your team will prove itself to be championship worthy.

As General Powell suggests, every leader must display a winning attitude regardless of circumstances. Often, circumstances are beyond your control. Your choice of attitude in the face of those circumstances, however, remains entirely your decision. Whether you are deployed in a combat area or working in a headquarters within the continental United States, a winning attitude multiplies your opportunities for success—and those of your unit.

Your own personal winning attitude begins with a look in the mirror. That person has the goods to be a winner! Created perfectly, you were placed on the earth to make a positive impact. You have a calling and unique abilities like no other. Let your winning attitude show in everything you do or say in the way you carry yourself and in the way you treat others.

Chapter 21

Perseverance

Keep calm and carry on.

—World War II-era slogan

Slogans have motivated entire nations.

"Keep calm and carry on" was printed on a poster distributed to British citizens prior to World War II. The message was intended to prepare them for the anticipated airstrikes of the war. It wasn't widely accepted at the time, but its message has survived to inspire members of today's military and their families.

The simplicity of the slogan is no indication of its timeless message. It is a call to persevere no matter what lies ahead. It is a message to troops about to be deployed, as well as a message to those left behind.

It says to all, "Don't let life's interruptions influence you to give up." Solomon, the wisdom writer in the Bible, said, "The race is not to the swift, nor the battle to the strong, neither yet bread to the wise, nor yet riches to men of understanding, nor yet favour to men of skill" (Ecclesiastes 9:11, KJV). Jesus completed the message hundreds of years later with the truth that the one who "endures to the end shall be saved" (Matthew 10:22, KJV).

Perseverance is waged in the trenches of life. It often experiences its loneliness and pain below deck—far away from the crowd. Its calm is deceiving, however. It draws uncommon strength from its determination to keep going, in spite of it all.

Are you ready to throw in the towel? Don't. Just stay calm, and carry on.

Chapter 22

Effort

The healthiest competition occurs
when average people win by putting
above average effort.

—General Colin Powell

What's the difference between first and second place? Effort! Extra effort wins games. It builds businesses. It amasses fortunes. It wins battles. The list goes on. Talent may be inherited, but effort is acquired. Talent may be revered, but effort is rewarded: To the victor go the spoils.

Effort is any behavior that is above average. It does more than expected, and it goes farther than necessary. It reaches higher and wider and digs deeper. It goes extra miles through uncharted waters. It plants flags at the summits of the tallest mountains.

You don't have to be a superstar to be a winner in the effort competition. You just have to be willing to sacrifice temporary comforts for long-term gains. You put something of yourself into everything you do. You don't have just your fingerprint on a project; your blood, sweat, or tears are also there.

The model for monumental effort is exemplified every day in VA hospitals or rehabilitation centers. It's in the eyes of wounded warriors who have paid a significant physical and mental price for the cause of liberty, and yet continue to strive to perfect a new normalcy.

Charles Shultz, author of the Peanuts cartoon, once said, "Life is like a ten-speed bike. Most of us have gears we never use." Test the limits of your capabilities. Give it all you've got for unit, service, and country.

Chapter 23

Grief

We should thank God

that such men lived.

—General George S. Patton

C asualties are the saddest fact of war.

Military personnel and their families must too often deal with the sad reality of a friend or loved one who has made the ultimate sacrifice. Graveside gun salutes and flag presentations are remembered to "Taps" echoing across the stillness.

Everyone handles grief at the loss of a son or daughter, sibling, father, or mother in a personal and unique way. Some express their anger at the circumstance, raging against the timing or the underlying conflict that caused the pain. Others openly weep over their loss. Still others grit their teeth with a steely determination to turn remembrance into resolve. One is not more normal than the others—and all represent the human sorrow that accompanies death.

The historically gruff World War II military hero calls us with his words to think of the fallen comrade not as one whose life was taken but rather to think of the comrade as one whose life was given. General Patton is suggesting a positive and more productive perspective on the reality of casualties. He is putting a soldier's ultimate sacrifice in the perspective of a greater purpose and noble calling.

The loss is real. The hurt is raw. But the brother or sister who has died has not died in vain. They have preserved liberty. They deserve, and we must express, the thanks of a grateful nation.

Chapter 24

Discipline

Discipline is the soul of the army. It

makes small numbers formidable;

procures success to the weak,

and esteem to all.

—General George Washington

Basic training might have been called basic discipline. It was that uncomfortable interval of time when you were being broken down for the purpose of being built up.

Pleases and thank-yous were noticeably absent in a drill instructor's native language. There was no room service, and housecleaning never called to see if you were satisfied with the way your room was kept.

You learned by adapting. You experienced the worst so you could become a proud member of the very best military in the world. Your combined training agonies formed you and your fellow recruits into a team like molten steel in a blazing fire. Diverse soldiers from across the country suddenly became like brothers and sisters.

The physical demands were great, but the mental demands were greater. Your mind-set was being rechanneled. You developed a winning attitude in the midst of your discomfort, and you learned to improvise, adapt, and overcome.

When it was all said and done, you were better. You learned that comfort is not a given in life. More importantly, you learned the criticality and value of military discipline. It ensures that execution of orders is prompt and instinctive. It makes success in battle possible even when facing significant odds. It results in individual and unit pride.

Discipline will be your friend for life. Use it to win. Use it when you fail. Use it in the face of adversity. Use it in the face of fear. It is the very soul of who you are as a soldier, sailor, airman, or marine.

Chapter 25

Humility

There is no limit to the good

you can do if you don't care

who gets the credit.

—General of the U.S. Army George C. Marshall

True humility is a character strength, but it usually flies under the radar. It isn't listed in your social media profile, and you never see it advertised in seminar brochures. There aren't many "humility specialists." Why? Humility is an attitude inadvertently—not purposely—shown through actions.

Humility is the "Aw, shucks!" factor that responds to a compliment. It deflects praise like a mirror pointed toward the sun. It wears kindness and respect for others like comfortable clothing. It also relieves pressure you might otherwise put on yourself by taking yourself too seriously.

Humility is a leadership trait as well. The most noted leaders aren't glory-seekers, they are glory-givers. Praise ricochets off them and hits those who serve under them. Because of humility, the wise leader is not position conscious. He or she intuitively understands that increased rank brings special responsibilities for others, service, and country—not special privilege.

Is it a learned characteristic? Yes, in some ways. First, begin with consciously remembering those who contributed to your own success. Praising them privately or publicly acknowledges their sacrificial effort. It also makes you grateful for others and puts your own life and role in perspective.

Second, make it a habit to give credit to others instead of keeping it. It will strengthen morale, and it will motivate to even greater achievement

Third, focus on team goals rather than personal goals. "We did it" is more important than "I did it by myself."

The paradox is that true humility is a character and leadership trait that will raise your esteem in the eyes of others.

Chapter 26

Strength

Let every nation know, whether it wishes us well or ill, that we shall pay any price, bear any burden, meet any hardship, support any friend, oppose any foe, to assure the survival and success of liberty.

—President John F. Kennedy

National strength is personal strength multiplied.

Nations aren't strong because of their bank holdings or their armament. They are strong because of the backbone of their citizenry. Strong people make strong choices borne of their strong values.

Have you ever thought of how many depend on you for protection and peace? Your ability and inner strength keep our country free. The chain of command is only as strong as its individual links. A weak link in the chain can impact an entire unit. One greedy person can betray his or her country for a sum far less than the cost of one weapon.

So be strong.

Be strong in character. Every single day you make moral decisions that determine your life and your career. Seek wise counsel. Consider the alternatives. Deny yourself immediate gratification if it threatens your long-term well-being and success. Choose your friends for who they are, not for what they can do. Conduct yourself honorably off duty as well as on. Take care of your family.

Be strong in mind. Despise the negative and love the positive. Refuse to believe your critics' assessment of you. Learn to listen for life tips. Fill your mind with good things.

Be strong in body. Make good decisions about what you eat or drink. Conquer habits that threaten your health. Exercise even when you're not told to.

Be strong enough to pay any price, bear any burden, meet any hardship, support any friend, oppose any foe.

Chapter 27

Persistence

In every battle there comes a time

when both sides consider themselves

beaten; then he who continues the

attack wins.

—General Ulysses S. Grant

Bethany Hamilton was not just any surfer.

Bethany will be forever known for what she became in spite of what happened to her.

In 2003, at the age of thirteen, she lost her left arm in a shark attack while surfing in Hawaii. By the time she reached the hospital, 60 percent of her blood had drained from her body. But Bethany not only survived but also thrived. Subject of scores of articles, several books, hundreds of media interviews, and the highly successful movie Soul Surfer, she refused to give up.

Within a month of her horrific injury, Bethany was back on the surfboard, pursuing her childhood pledge to be a professional surfer. Just one year later she won a national championship, and in 2007, she became a professional surfer. Giving credit to her faith in God, Bethany has inspired millions to never quit, to never give up.

Similarly, in the military, persistence is a vital leadership and character trait. The military life brings with it innumerable challenges and difficulties. Persistence may be defined as firmly continuing in a correct course of action in spite of difficulty or opposition. As General Grant suggests, persistence may very well prove a decisive factor in achieving success in battle. And persistence may give you that added edge to achieve your personal goal.

Leaders set the example for persistence. In October 1941, when Great Britain stood virtually alone against the Axis powers, Winston Churchill said, "Never, never, in nothing great or small, large or petty, never give in, except to convictions of honour and good sense." You, too, can set the tone to never given in and never give up.

Chapter 28

Ethic

You should do your duty in all things.
You can never do more. You should
never wish to do less.

—General Robert E. Lee

Everyone has an ethic, a personal standard for behavior. What is your work ethic? Which of the following ideals influence that area of your life?

Take it or leave it.

That's good enough.

Finish the job.

Can do.

Honesty is the best policy.

It doesn't even have to be spoken, but it drives or slows your work. You either excel or get by, based on your inner belief toward what you do.

The Civil War general nailed it: You can never do more . . . you should never do less.

Call it a standard of excellence, or give it another name; it is the stuff of honor—the crown of victory—or the agony of defeat. Doing one's duty is a cornerstone value of those in the military.

If you have to be driven, one could assume that you have no drive. But if you work as hard when you're alone as you do when others are around, one could assume that you have a solid work ethic.

Maybe you haven't thought much about it. Maybe you just do what you do and wait for the paycheck. It's time to give it some thought. Too much depends on it. Too many depend on it.

Start with putting in a full day's work. Put your heart into your work. If it's not all there now, it soon will be. Practice to do the best you can do, and you'll soon be doing it.

Chapter 29

Patriotism

I was summoned by my country,

whose voice I can never hear but with

veneration and love.

—President George Washington

Patriotism flows through your veins, silently and solemnly.

Choosing to defend your country for financial benefits wouldn't keep you beyond the first deployment. Something greater must drive you to make a military career your cause. It is love and devotion for your country.

Patriotism is the stirring that occurs on sight of the beautiful red, white, and blue United States flag waving before you. It is a profound and enduring appreciation of our country's ideals that the flag represents. It includes a deep and abiding respect for all those who have served, bled, and died to defend our country.

The latter is particularly meaningful to those serving in the military. You don't have to be a history buff to learn about the great battles that have been won on land, sea, and air. You just have to be a learner. Each battle is a lesson to be learned. Each records failures as well as victories; and knowing their history may keep you from repeating the failures and enable you to achieve future victories. What you learn about those who have carved the paths of yesterday will help you be the leader and defender our country needs today and tomorrow. Your country has summoned you—answer with the best you have to offer.

In that world-acclaimed 2013 photo of wounded U.S. Army Ranger Cpl. Josh Hargis raising a bandaged arm to salute his commander in chief during a Purple Heart ceremony, you probably saw that he was on a breathing tube. That one action said more about patriotism than ten thousand words could ever say.

Chapter 30

Courtesy

It is an old and a true maxim, that a
"drop of honey catches more flies than
a gallon of gall." So, with men.

—President Abraham Lincoln

C ourtesy pays far more dividends than it costs.

Military customs and courtesies are time-honored traditions for showing honor and respect within the profession of arms. Among other things, they serve as a distinctive and valuable means of helping instill discipline, pride, and esprit de corps among men and women in uniform. Common courtesy focuses primarily on politeness. It is demonstrated by showing kindness, civility, and grace. The value of common courtesy as a leadership and character trait, both within and outside the military, goes unrecognized too often.

Military leaders have the ability to command others to follow them or obey their command because of rank and the Uniform Code of Military Justice (UCMJ). However, reliance on those as a first resort is a failure of leadership. Lincoln's adage about using a drop of honey to catch men is simply another way of saying that kindness and politeness is a superior means for leading and influencing people.

Common courtesy means to focus on others rather than self. It allows persons to discuss differences person to person rather than by innuendo or rumor. It allows us to apologize without hesitation when an apology is appropriate. Common courtesy is at work when we acknowledge the efforts of subordinates and remember personnel milestones. It causes us to question without arrogance or haughtiness and to avoid email wars. Your predetermination to remain courteous helps you hold your own thought when it is appropriate to listen rather than speaking your mind. A courteous person treats everyone with respect, because each individual is of great worth.

Common courtesy is a plus for almost every aspect of your life. It is exceptionally valuable in dealing with superiors, peers, subordinates, and when working out difficult inter-organizational issues. It will help make you a standout leader.

Chapter 31

Resolve

Progress occurs when courageous,

skillful leaders seize the opportunity to

change things for the better.

—President Harry Truman

One of the most powerful words in the English language has only two letters: NO.

The problem with an anything-goes culture is that one of its first losses is personal security. Most often, the word no is a security fence. Granted, sometimes no is sharp and harmful, like the rolled barbwire of most security fences. But it wasn't built for comfort, it was built for control.

Interestingly, children who are born into families with no curfews often feel more unloved and insecure than those born into families with enforced curfews. Boundaries actually feed our feelings of safety. We think, Someone cares enough about my safety to set protective rules.

A military leader must be resolute in accomplishing the mission, goal, or objective. Sometimes this means the leader must demonstrate the judgment and moral courage to just say no. No doesn't mean maybe. No certainly means defining the limits of acceptable personal behavior. In other words, it is applicable in everyday military decision making, but also highly important in combat settings.

Spaghetti-spine leadership is dangerous. It allows troops to follow whims or feelings rather than the mission. Thinking approval will be won by allowance, a leader ultimately discovers that the opposite is true.

It may be the most challenging decision you will make, but changing your attitude about the value of the word no will make you a better soldier, sailor, airman, or marine—and ultimately a better leader.

Chapter 32

Purpose

My own definition of leadership is
this: The capacity and the will to rally
men and women to a common purpose
and the character which inspires
confidence.

—Field Marshal Bernard Law Montgomery

At about the age of three, children begin to ask why, and for the next year or so that question becomes the supply line in every conversation.

It may be that we never outgrow that question. Maybe it is an anchor for our behavior or the drive train for our beliefs. We may never be content without an answer. The answer is our purpose—the reason we do things.

Field Marshal Montgomery, the World War II British military commander, regarded purpose as the pinion of all military leadership, the "common purpose and the character which inspires confidence."

Our purpose takes us to our destination. We can have the most luxurious automobile in the neighborhood, but it's useless without an engine. We can push it or tow it to the point of exhaustion, but it is still worthless to us without a motor.

Purpose is the motor that empowers you to reach your personal destination. Purpose can also be corporate. Troops together have a common purpose—the mission. They join their capacities and wills together to meet goals and objectives. That's where you come in. First, it's your job to identify the mission, whether it comes from your superiors or is self-propelled. You must learn to understand the mission well enough to write it down in a few sentences.

Second, it's your responsibility to communicate it clearly. Each person must understand how his or her role contributes to the success of the overall mission. Third, it's your job to make sure your subordinates stay on-mission—heading in the right direction on the right schedule.

Chapter 33

Influence

The greatness of a leader is measured

by the achievements of the led.

—General Omar Bradley

A cartoon shows a sailor giving a tour. He stops under an impressive painting of a U.S. Navy officer on which the caption reads: "That's our beloved Admiral. He drowned in a sea of red tape."

If someone painted your picture, what would the caption say about you? That question might make all of us a bit nervous, but it provokes some thought. All of us are known by something we have said or done, and after we are gone that influence will continue, though there will probably be a few addendums.

You are leaving footprints that the winds of time will not soon cover. And like it or not, someone will examine those prints and make a decision whether or not to walk in those steps. Your first concern, then, is to lead, serve, and live a life in a manner worthy of following.

Your second concern is to duplicate the best you have to offer in the life of another. In simplest terms, you must be a mentor to develop those you lead.

Mentoring is a noble but humbling responsibility. Leaders of the next generation are looking for traits and tools from today's leaders to emulate. Scary, isn't it? But think of how you learned to lead. You are probably following a leader. You have noted the best practices of someone who had authority over you, and you are reproducing that person in your own leadership.

So, remember: Someone is watching—and following—you.

Chapter 34

Risk

It was faith and belief;

it was loyalty and love.

—President Ronald Reagan

During the fortieth commemoration of D-Day, President Ronald Reagan answered his own rhetorical question about what causes military service members to risk life and limb. He said, "It was faith and belief; it was loyalty and love."

Military leaders serve for reasons that are bigger than themselves. They understand the deep foundational reasons men and women risk everything to serve—especially during combat. It is not for glory; glory isn't on someone's mind when he or she is sweeping an area for improvised explosive devices. That person is focused on survival and the survival of the members of the unit.

In fact, it's doubtful that any military hero imagined his or her name inscribed on a monument when under enemy fire. Glory didn't embed the hero in the battle; it was something deeper and wider than that. It was love of country and everything it stands for. It was a principle worthy of protecting with life itself.

From the moment you raised your hand of allegiance and vowed to support and defend the Constitution of the United States against all enemies, foreign and domestic, you knew there would be risks involved.

Everything of worth begins with risk; risk goes with the territory. It is the launching pad for trial and error. Take it, and you will probably be out of your comfort zone. But you must take it in order to make a greater contribution to your unit and your service.

Chapter 35

Adversity

Be thankful for problems. If they were less difficult, someone with less ability might have your job.

—Captain James A. Lovell, NASA Astronaut

When Oklahoma World War II veteran Phillip Coon received a Prisoner of War Medal from Major General Rita Aragon, he said, "I've been blessed to come this far in life. I thank the Lord for watching over me." The ninety-four-year-old survived a POW labor camp and the Bataan Death March that killed eleven thousand soldiers.

Your survivor story may or may not be equally momentous, but if you have served any time in the military, you have confronted and survived adversity. And you, too, can say, "I'm blessed to come this far." You are a member of a not-so-elite club that has taken on adversity and won.

Adversity can take many forms. Perhaps it is the day when everything that can possibly go wrong at the office did go wrong. Perhaps you are the subject of unjust criticism or accusation. How do you respond?

Embrace the challenge of problems. Take the view that your superiors chose you for this role for a reason. They believed you were a problem-solver and could successfully tackle the issues at hand.

Believe in yourself and your team. Have confidence in your own abilities, and leverage the abilities of others.

Stick with it. Albert Einstein once said, "It's not that I'm so smart, it's just that I stay with problems longer."

If your life is a life of ease, somebody with less experience and ability may get the job.

Chapter 36

Planning

If we should have to fight, we should
be prepared to do so from the neck up
instead of the neck down.

—General James H. Doolittle

Plan your work, and work your plan.

The saying comes from the 1880s and was written by Source Unknown, the most quoted author on the planet. Whoever said it first had the right idea, and the truth of it never gets rusty. Military leaders understand the value of adding planning time to their calendars.

General Dwight D. Eisenhower gave the saying an interesting spin, "In preparing for battle I have always found that plans are useless, but planning is indispensable." Some plans fail on day one, and are discarded at first contact. The variables change. The adversaries' capability or intent may prove different than believed. Perhaps the weather changes rapidly or the terrain is more challenging. The fog and friction of war will always stress well-conceived plans. But the situation would be catastrophic if plan B wasn't already unfolding. One of the benefits of planning is the ability to think through and prepare for various contingencies.

Thomas Edison may be the king of plan B as evidenced by one of his frequently quoted theories: "I have not failed. I've just found 10,000 ways that won't work." You can be sure that between 10,000 and 10,001, there was some serious thinking going on.

There is too much at stake to not plan; too many lives stand to be affected. Playing it by ear and dealing with situations as they occur is risky at best and catastrophic at worst.

Take control of your calendar. Set aside time to think and plan. You can get there from here.

Chapter 37

Responsibility

I will work. I will save. I will sacrifice.

I will endure. I will fight cheerfully

and do my utmost, as if the issue

of the whole struggle depended

on me alone.

—Private Martin A. Treptow,
From the diary entry of
this World War I hero killed in France

I t's okay to have nothing to do, just don't be doing it around here," the commander said to considerable laughter from his troops.

Laziness in the military not only is futile but also can be fatal. The ability to take personal responsibility for your actions is among the strongest of character traits—and particularly highly valued in the military. Private Treptow's pledge, quoted in President Ronald Reagan's first inaugural address, is a primetime example of accepting personal responsibility. "As if the whole struggle depended on me alone. . . ."

Remember the very first time you accepted responsibility? It may have been when you were first asked to take out the trash. Or it may have been when you were appointed "Official Board Eraser" in grade school. Was it in high school when you were first handed the car keys? If you are a parent, it was definitely that moment when you held your newborn in your arms.

Taking responsibility in the military brings a level of commitment that makes heroes out of ordinary citizens. Responsibility requires dedication. Responsibility requires sacrifice. Responsibility is giving your utmost—your very best effort. Responsibility illustrates the importance of every person's effort in a military service.

Private Treptow left his job in a small-town barber shop to become a member of the famed Rainbow Division. He died in France while trying to carry a message between battalions under heavy artillery fire. Fortunately, most will never be required to duplicate his sacrifice, but all should duplicate his example of dedication and personal responsibility.

Take responsibility. Someone needs what only you can do.

Chapter 38

Excellence

The power of excellence is overwhelming. It is always in demand and nobody cares about its color.

—General Daniel S. "Chappie" James,
first African-American to become a four-star general

S ears stores were among the first to price their products according to good, better, or best.

If you bought a good cooking stove, for example, you probably paid the lowest price for the fewest bells and whistles. In contrast, if you bought the best, you paid the highest price, and it might have cooked dinner by itself and called you at work when it was done. That may be an exaggeration, but the bottom line is, you got what you paid for.

NBA star Tim Duncan quotes the tweaked version in a phrase that has motivated him from childhood, "Good, better, best . . . never let it rest, until your good is better and your better is your best."

Aim for excellence. There are plenty of folks who make it a habit to settle for good and better. Getting by doesn't help you get ahead. You get ahead by giving everything you do your best effort.

On the job, do more than you are asked to do; stay longer than you need to. Give more than necessary. Over-prepare. Aim for perfection. If you are known for getting by, your supervisors may pass you by.

In leadership, expect excellence from those you supervise. Don't reward sloppiness; it will only multiply sloppy effort while discouraging your top performers. Set the excellence standard.

Chapter 39

Discernment

Strange as it sounds, great leaders gain

authority by giving it away.

—Admiral James B. Stockdale

L eaders are known by the companies they keep.

In most cases, military leaders don't have a choice in company. They face the task of building community, team spirit, and loyalty from a group of imperfect strangers. And often they are called on to make split-second decisions with little or no information and then execute those decisions with whom they are assigned in an unknown environment.

In other cases, leaders are able to choose those who will oversee the key components of a mission or task. Good leaders have good discernment. They retain the best people, and perhaps most important, give them enough slack to bring their talents and creativity to the surface. They judge the strengths and weaknesses of their team and train the team members accordingly.

Discernment is important in all areas of life, but especially in interpersonal relationships. You know the importance of choosing the right people. Choosing the wrong friends and associates can have a negative effect on your whole life. Putting the wrong person in charge of a mission can cause a litany of problems.

Deliberate attention feeds discernment. What your team members say helps you understand how they feel. And how they feel is influenced by where they have been—or what has happened to them.

- Listen for the catch-phrases.
- Watch for immediate reactions.
- Notice ongoing interests.
- Consider networks.
- Learn each individual's unique strengths.

Choose who will share your authority—and then give it as needed.

Chapter 40

Family

When you lose your men, and you
carry them off the battlefield, bearing
a terrible truth that would tear the lives
and hearts of their families in 24 to 48
hours, when they got the telegram, it
gets to you. You feel guilty that you're
still alive.

—Lt. Gen. Harold G. Moore

Military leaders have two families: theirs and the families of those they lead.

Leaders care for the family as well as the soldier. Nothing happens to them that does not affect you as well. When you set out to mold a disparate group of individuals into a winning team, you must understand that their life dynamics become a part of yours.

Unless you have somehow developed a heart of steel and the emotions of a brick, you will weep with those who weep and rejoice with those who rejoice. Your reaction won't always be open or public, but the inner burdens of your team are inner burdens to you.

How you treat that family in times of crisis will tag you as a leader. Cold indifference in the eyes of those you lead will stay with you like a gray cloud. Conversely, warm concern will enhance the esteem with which you are held.

Of course, your own family is a constant concern. Parents, siblings, spouse, or children are on your priority list—or should be. Your attitudes and actions influence them even more than they influence your team. You relate to them at eye-level. Your rank will mean far less to them than your reach.

Family matters matter.

Chapter 41

Recovery

Hindsight is notably cleverer

than foresight.

—Fleet Admiral of the U.S. Navy Chester Nimitz

Military leaders bounce back.

There are nearly forty thousand Likes on the Facebook page of the USS Nimitz. The U.S. Navy aircraft carrier is part of the "Nimitz Class," a group of ten nuclear-powered carriers. It was named after Fleet Admiral of the U.S. Navy Chester Nimitz. Why is that significant? As an ensign, Chester Nimitz was conning the destroyer USS Decatur when it ran aground on a sandbar in 1908. Nimitz was court-martialed, found guilty of neglect of duty, and issued a letter of reprimand.

One year later, he was transferred to the submarine service. In 1911, Chester Nimitz was named commander, 3rd Submarine Division Atlantic Torpedo Fleet. In 1918, he received a letter of commendation for his leadership during World War I. And the rest is an honorable history.

One misstep didn't sink Admiral Nimitz. He bounced back with a service to his country that very few ever dreamed possible — especially those who served on the military court that reprimanded him.

You may not have steered a destroyer into a sandbar. Your misstep may have been a step below a misdemeanor, but you know how it messed with your mind. The good news is that you can make a comeback. Hindsight is not your friend, so why spend time with it? Change direction; start over. Make peace with God and others. Clear the slate and throw away the permanent marker.

The military may not honor you by naming an aircraft carrier after you, but you can discover the same peace of mind that a fleet admiral of the navy found. Bounce back. Use the experience to become a better, stronger leader than ever before.

Chapter 42

Details

Never neglect details.

When everyone's mind is dulled

or distracted, the leader must be

doubly vigilant.

—General Colin Powell

Beware of the so-called experts with twenty-five years of experience and ten minutes of knowledge.

Campaigns are won or lost over attention to details. Leaders delegate, but they must also pay attention to details every day. This ensures that organizational routine doesn't result in complacency, and ultimately the loss of operational effectiveness.

What if an aircraft mechanic assumes the aircraft has been inspected before flight when it hasn't? Not only might it result in a potentially fatal incident, air operations could temporarily grind to a halt as investigators search for the cause.

If you will be a master of anything militarily, be a master of details. The buck stops at your desk. Checklists are your friends. Calendars are your buddies. Walk around and ask questions. Relentlessly follow-up on the progress of tasks well before they are due.

The success of your task may very well affect overall mission or project success. If you drop the ball, the battle may be lost or the project derailed.

Details, details, details!

Chapter 43

Audacity

I wish to have no connection with any ship that does not sail fast, for I intend to go in harm's way.

—John Paul Jones,
officer of the Continental Navy of the American Revolution

Some military decisions simply won't wait for intricate operational and resource allocation planning. They must be made immediately and precisely — short and fast. Audacity is that bold and adventuresome spirit that says, "Let's go! Now is as good a time as any."

Audacity can enable a leader to exploit an opportunity to maximum advantage. Audacious action can also inspire.

During World War II, an American P-51 pilot named William Overstreet Jr. flew his plane under the Eiffel Tower while in hot pursuit of an enemy plane. He not only successfully downed the enemy aircraft, but his daring and aggressive action inspired the French resistance on the ground in Nazi-occupied Paris.

Audacity is characterized by daring, but it is daring that is founded on confidence and a thorough understanding of conflict and its potential consequences. It is carried out with an air of decisiveness.

The leader who acts audaciously recognizes that not every situation gives way to a carefully calculated, logical, and pragmatically determined solution. Some problems will yield only to daring, bold, and decisive action.

Sometimes you must, literally or figuratively, pull the trigger and then adjust fire. When the situation warrants it, be aggressive. Take audacious action.

Chapter 44

Impact

Some people live their entire lifetime
and wonder if they ever made a
difference to the world. Marines don't
have that problem.

—President Ronald Reagan

When you take a look at the biographies of the rich and famous, you won't find a lot of slacking off. People don't reach the next level by camping at the first. They determine to be high impact—the fastest, smartest, strongest, or ablest on the planet—and they are willing to pay the price to get there. As legendary basketball coach John Wooden said, "Success travels in the company of very hard work."

Have you thought about what impact your life will have? What have you determined to do that will make a difference to the world? You may be thinking, There are 7 billion people in the world, what can I possibly do to make a difference?

First, you are already impacting your country and beyond by your service. Your daily actions help protect your fellow citizens. Your military service makes the blessings of freedom possible not only here but in many other areas of the world as well. Determine to do it diligently—knowing that the freedom you help secure improves the lives of many others.

Second, you have the ability to impact your world—your military base, your community, your family and friends—by the way you do life. Do it purposefully and courageously; intend to make a positive impact.

Make the conscious decision to be high-impact. Work hard. Be aggressive in accomplishing or improving things. Tackle issues larger than your inbox. Invest in the lives of others. Lend a helping hand, on and off duty.

Chapter 45

Faith

Military power wins battles,

but spiritual power wins wars.

—General George Marshall

People who don't have faith shouldn't have a driver's license. Driving, especially these days, is potentially hazardous. Consider that you may be facing another driver with a smartphone in one hand, a cheeseburger in the other, and hot coffee in the console. Add to the fact that Driver A is also trying to listen to a favorite song while untangling earbuds and dodging orange cones, and you realize that your step into your vehicle is actually a leap of faith.

Fact is, you can't drive without a belief system.

- You believe the door will unlock when you push the remote button.
- You believe there is enough fuel in the gas tank to get you to your destination.
- You believe the engine will start when you turn the key in the ignition.
- You believe the electrical and mechanical systems will work in sync.
- You believe the traffic lights will function.
- You believe the drivers in the oncoming traffic know how to drive.

Something deep within causes you to trust engineers, manufacturers, and law enforcement enough to put your life in their hands. Similarly, you face the challenges of military life with an inner belief that all systems are go. You reach into the very core of yourself and hold on to a power greater than you for wisdom and power. That is faith, made from a decision to go forward in spite of the obstacles or dangers.

Chapter 46

Flexibility

The value of the individual increases

in a time of resource constraints.

—Air Force General Edward Rice

I talian General and airpower theorist Guilio Douhet was probably the first to say, "Flexibility is the key to airpower." The truth is that flexibility is a key to success in many military endeavors. Military personnel are taught early on that they must improvise, adapt, and overcome. They must do what they can do with what they have on hand—especially in combat—but also during peace in an era of budget restraints.

Learned flexibility is a survival skill. It is also a leadership trait.

Learning to be flexible includes understanding yourself. Your background influences your foreground. You have your way of doing things based on what you observed and what you discovered.

Learning to be flexible includes understanding others. Each individual is unique, bringing unique talents, abilities, methods, and personalities. Every person is a product of his or her own background and experiences.

Learning to be flexible includes understanding how to be resourceful with equipment and assets. During the Apollo 13 crisis, flight director Gene Kranz reflected this skill when he declared, "I don't care about what anything was designed to do, I care about what it can do."

Merging knowledge of yourself with knowledge of others, and combining that with resourceful and innovative use of assets, will mark you as an all-star performer.

Chapter 47

Values

In an era of unprecedented change,

now more than ever, we need to

continually renew our commitment to

the institution and the values that set

us apart.

—Lt. Gen. Richard P. Mills,
Commander of Marine Forces Reserve and Marine Forces North

Military life is a system. Systems may be defined as organized principles and procedures working together for a common purpose. At their very core are shared beliefs—enduring values that motivate the decisions and actions of all those that serve in the organization. Service core values form the basis of military leadership.

Military leaders must adhere to the values of their branch of service. For example, Semper Fidelis (always faithful) is a reminder of a marine's pledge to live by the standards of the corps. Military leaders also have personal values that reinforce service values, such as Duty, Honor, Country.

- Personal values drive loyalty, service, and a standard for excellence.
- Personal values prevent excess or abuse.
- Personal values set parameters of acceptable behavior.

Strong or weak, your values shape your character. You are what you believe.

A customer viewed a product description in an electronics store. "This is an all-purpose remote." The customer commented to the salesperson, "I have four kids. My chances of controlling that TV are already remote!"

Likewise, the chances of exemplary behavior in a changing culture without a personal code of behavior are already remote. So, how is a value system formed or strengthened?

First, strengthen your faith. Religious belief influences secular actions.

Second, study iconic leaders from all walks of life as well as contemporary leaders that you admire. Learn from the best of the best.

Third, follow your heart—your own deeply held sense of honor. If something doesn't feel right, it probably isn't right.

Chapter 48

Readiness

The U.S. Coast Guard's motto is

Semper Paratus, meaning

Always Ready.

Support your local Coast Guard—Get Lost!

That humorous saying may be an unintentional branding, but its underlying message, which is that the coast guard will be there when you need it most, is right on target. The Homeland Security and Department of Defense branch of service may be smaller in size than other branches of service, but its responsibility is great. In peacetime, it aids shipping, patrols national borders, conducts search and rescue operations, and prevents smuggling. In wartime, it is ready to assist the U.S. Navy in national defense.

The U.S. Coast Guard has maritime and air stations alongside oceans, lakes, and rivers where crews stand ready to risk their lives to save the lives of others. The institutional readiness of the U.S. Coast Guard, and all the military services, is constantly measured and evaluated.

Personal readiness is both a mind-set and a leadership skill. It springs into action on instinct, based on prior training and experience.

Military leaders are always personally ready. They maintain their physical, spiritual, and mental fitness to better meet the inevitable stress of military service. They are well-schooled in their profession. They have trained, exercised, and engaged in countless tabletop scenarios over the years. As a result, they have planned responses, as well as an experience base to respond decisively to unanticipated events. They don't panic; they react out of experience. They respond to critical circumstances with outer calmness in spite of inner concern. They are alert, consider the crisis, and respond appropriately, quickly, and carefully.

This is an age when our country faces traditional, persistent, and newly emerging unconventional threats. Institutional military readiness is critical to meeting these threats, as is the personal readiness of each individual service member. Set the standard for personal readiness and steadiness.

Chapter 49

Hope

A leader is a dealer in hope.

—Napoleon Bonaparte

An art collector was showing a friend through her home in which expensive works of art by well-known artists were displayed. The visitor asked, "Which is your favorite?" The art collector took her to the kitchen and pointed to a piece of lined paper that had been torn from a writing pad. On it was what seemed to be a flower and some words scrawled in purple crayon, To the best Mommy. "This one is priceless," she said.

Nearly every day of your military career you will meet someone who needs an encouraging word. Some have been told they are worthless and battle self-esteem issues. Some bear scars on the outside that are minor in comparison to those on the inside. Others give every outward appearance that everything is just fine, while inwardly they are battling hidden discouragement and doubt. Sadly, the military services struggle with substance abuse and outsized suicide rates as a result of these and other issues.

Soldiers, sailors, airmen, and marines need hope. They need to know they have ability and potential. They need to know that someone has their "six"—that someone is on their side.

As a leader, you have the incomparable opportunity to give them the priceless treasures of affirmation and encouragement. From time to time, you may have to sandwich a positive word between a command or correction, but the effort will pay in ways you may never know. Mark Twain once illustrated the power of encouragement when he said, "I can live for two months on a good compliment."

Find ways to let your subordinates know that you believe in them. You will see tangible results in improved morale, heightened performance, commitment, loyalty, dedication, and esprit de corps. So, be generous with hope and encouragement. Do it today.

Chapter 50

Loyalty

I can't expect loyalty from the army

if I do not give it.

—George C. Marshall,
U.S. Secretary of Defense and Army Chief of Staff

White House Chief of Staff Donald Regan once said, "You've got to give loyalty down, if you want loyalty up."

Leadership is like a ladder, worthless at any level unless it is on solid ground and leaning against something. And those who climb its rungs are at greater risk the higher they climb if no one is holding it steady. The ladder-holders are subordinates who are loyal to their leadership.

Loyalty from leadership to the led is demonstrated by using one's rank and influence to serve others and the organization. That includes giving credit when things go well and taking the heat when things go wrong.

Loyalty is one of the more important character traits for those in the armed forces. It begins in your heart, the command center of your emotions. It is an emotional or intellectual bond formed with another person, mission, or cause.

How do you recognize loyalty?

Loyalty is demonstrated with commitment. The willingness to defend your organization and those in it is a noble quality.

Loyalty means to be always faithful. Count saluting as a privilege. Voice significant disagreements or correction privately.

- Loyalty is built by teamwork and is a bond formed by friendly, cooperative relationships and strengthened during shared adversity.

- Loyalty is expressed in service as you commit time and energy and endure untold hardships.

- Loyalty is displayed by remaining true to your beliefs and those serving alongside you.

Both you and your organization win with loyalty.

Chapter 51

Thought

Take calculated risks. That is quite
different from being rash.

—General George S. Patton, Jr.

How's your thought life?

That's not one of your everyday questions. We usually give more attention to doing and being rather than thinking. Our conversations focus on such things as skills, relationships, careers, finances, or health. But seldom do we talk about our CPU, our central processing unit—the brain.

Successful or failed missions begin with thought—or the absence of it. The mind processes confidence, skill, capability, education, and experience, and then sends green or red alerts that influence actions.

The thoughtful military leader is capable of realizing the maximum value of risk precisely because he or she is able to calculate the benefits and risks of the action based on sound and educated reasoning. Sound reasoning filters out selfish or emotional thoughts. Educated reasoning filters in past experience or classroom learning. Pure thought is the result—thought that is an enabling factor for success.

Pure thought is also deliberate focusing on components as well as the whole.

Pure thought does not succumb to emotion. Another World War II military leader, Admiral Chester Nimitz, put it this way, "God gave us two ends to think with; heads we win, tails we lose."

The difficulty for military leaders is that too often the more significant the responsibility and scope of authority, the less time there is for thought. For that reason, it is vital to set aside some time for reading and thinking.

Learning to think things through is a key to success in any field, but especially in the military. Your thoughts could save a life or win a battle.

Chapter 52

Perspective

I like the dreams of the future better

than the history of the past.

—Thomas Jefferson

Military leaders value history and its lessons—but they keep their eyes on the horizon and anticipate future possibilities.

Robert Kennedy said, "Some men see things as they are and ask why; I dream things that never were and ask why not." Perspective is one factor that separates high-profile leaders from others. Some leaders can't see the sun for the clouds, while others can't see the clouds for the sun. Their futures are bright, because their perspective is positive.

In some ways, perspective is contagious. Your family of origin had a way of seeing things. They were either glass-half-empty thinkers or glass-half-full thinkers. As an adult, your circle of friends has a perspective that will also influence you. It's time to gain a personal perspective.

Focus on the dreams of the future instead of the history of the past. Nurture a hopeful perspective; look for the positive aspects of the bad situation. Keep your eyes on the finish line rather than the hurdles. Talk the talk, and soon you will walk the walk.

Surround yourself with the positives. Choose your reading material carefully, hang with positive people, keep first things first. Take care to spend time with positive friends and family and refuse to dwell on the negative.

In turn, be a positive influence. Help others to dream big. Have a vision that will inspire others, and foster organizational spirit and pride. Encourage your team to take leaps of faith rather than the cautious steps of doubt.

Chapter 53

Opinion

If it is good to say or do something,

then it is even better to be criticized for

having said or done it.

—Marcus Aurelius, Roman Emperor

Decide which font style describes you best: BOLD, italics, or normal.

Are you normally afraid to speak your mind or are you quick to boldly share your opinion? Are you straight up about your beliefs or do you slant them in an attempt to avoid criticism and get everyone to like you?

During the 2013 NFL season, a controversy over bullying arose. When a member of one team was disciplined for his words about another, other players took sides. One spoke for league disciplinary action, citing past bullying episodes. In the process he told of an extreme hazing incident that he had witnessed.

He said when he came into the room and saw the plight of a rookie player that was being tormented, he knew he had to risk speaking up. "This has to stop now!" he shouted. He was criticized, but it led to measures that restricted the severity of rookie hazing incidents.

An opinion can be like an exploding grenade or a refreshing rainstorm complete with the thunder and lightning. The difference is in the situation, the timing, and the delivery; all three coming from your knowledge and experience.

General Norman Schwarzkopf said, "The truth of the matter is that you always know the right thing to do. The hard part is doing it." Military leaders have the moral courage to speak up for the right things, even if that results in disagreement or criticism. Their intellect, judgment, conscience, and loyalty guide them. They say the right things and they say the right things the right way.

Chapter 54

Vision

The task of the leader is to get his people from where they are to where they have not been.

—Henry Kissinger, former U.S. Secretary of State

There is a saying among some in the military: "If it ain't broke, don't fix it." That is simply wrong to the extent that it encourages resting on the status quo.

The visionary leader recognizes that the pace of change is so significant in the modern era that if an organization ever stops improving, it will become comparatively less capable as time passes. As American humorist Will Rogers said, "Even if you are on the right track, you will get run over if you just sit there."

The visionary leader begins by communicating a desired destination for the organization and does so in a transparent manner. He or she speaks with conviction, invites ideas, and welcomes feedback, because he or she understands the power this has to inspire those in the organization.

Visionary leaders promote change only within the context of moving toward an identifiable future destination. They never promote change for the sake of change. They understand that few things are more annoying to those in the military than someone who changes something for no apparent purpose. And they know that moving around a few organizational line and block charts is likely to produce more upheaval than progress.

The visionary leader values the very best of military history and heritage while striving for future possibilities. He or she may very well see their vision within the context of its most valuable principles and most reliable doctrine.

Visionary military leaders are never content with the status quo. They inspire their organization and people forward to new achievements.

Chapter 55

Gossip

Great minds discuss ideas,

average minds discuss events,

small minds discuss people.

—Admiral Hyman G. Rickover

Gossip is retelling supposed truth to supposedly honest people who will supposedly keep it to themselves.

Even after telegraph, telephone, and telecommunications, tell-a-friend is still the fastest way to send people news around the block and around the world. Scandal magazines have capitalized on people's need to know with stories of dubious origin.

Gossip columnists may come and go, but gossip still thrives as long as people continue to circulate half-truths and edited truth in public or private. Don't join their union. It's not only a perfect waste of the English language but also an incendiary action that could blow a career out of the water. Even worse, gossip is a verifiable weapon of mass destruction for organizational cohesion.

There are at least five good reasons why leaders should avoid it like Dengue Fever.

- It is totally unprofessional. As a leader, you are a standard-bearer. Gossip doesn't raise the standard, it lowers it.

- It is dangerous to troop morale. Rumor divides the very people you need to perform in unity.

- It marks the gossiper as unreliable. Gossip sabotages trust in leadership.

- It can be fatal to the person targeted. People crippled by rumor and false accusation often choose suicide to deal with their despair.

- It lowers your self-esteem. You never feel better about yourself after you have belittled another.

Spend your time telling about the good in people. If you do, you won't have time to repeat rumors about the bad.

Chapter 56

Procrastination

The difficult we do immediately; the
impossible takes a little longer.

— Air Force Motto

Procrastination isn't just a time waster; it's a potential career breaker.

Which would you choose to complete your mission: a chronic procrastinator or a can-do, get-'er-done type? The latter is clearly the go-to team. Not only do procrastinators drag their feet, but they usually put a drag on the entire mission.

Worse, procrastination is contagious. Failure to act promptly can negatively influence others involved in the mission. And like anything that is contagious, if it isn't cured, it gets progressively worse.

So, why might you procrastinate? Perhaps you are assigned an arduous task with significant hurdles; or you may be called on to make a tough and potentially unpopular decision. It may be that you must confront difficult or unproductive personnel. It may be that fear of failure is causing indecision.

If you want to progress as a leader, don't put the challenging tasks off. Start a project well in advance of its due date, break it down into achievable components, and check off action steps as you progress. Don't hesitate to make the call when you know what must be done on a personnel issue. Go into attack-mode on your most difficult challenges.

Military leaders are take-charge people. They see a need, assess it, and go to work meeting it—without unnecessary hesitation. But urgency is no substitute for efficiency. Think before you act, and act according to your knowledge, training, and experience.

Most of your effort will be in the area of the possible; do it right away. If you are called to do the so-called impossible, start right away and keep moving to completion. Be aggressive in tackling the problem before the problem tackles you.

Chapter 57

Diversity

One of our greatest advantages is our
diversity. This is an advantage we
should capitalize on across
all platforms.

—Secretary of the U.S. Navy Ray Mabus

People are the same, differently.

Diversity is a common theme these days. However, the conversation must begin with a common premise: The human race has different styles and colors, but under the hood, we are all the same.

Another premise is that diversity isn't just about skin color. It has to do with the entire personality, including natural abilities and learned skills. For example, a unit may be sent on a mission, and from its uniforms you could tell which branch of the military it represents. But that sight picture is no indication of the diverse individual capabilities, skills, and talents represented.

For some troops, appreciating diversity represents a sizable learning curve. For others, it's a given. The difference may relate to upbringing or some unpleasant interpersonal experience. In some ways, none of us ever leave home. We bring it with us—with all of its personal dynamics.

The military does a wonderful job of bringing people together from all nationalities, races, religions, and socioeconomic backgrounds, providing them with a common training environment and molding them into one team. It puts its trust in team abilities rather than individual peculiarities. Every person in the military, regardless of background, contributes to the cause.

Diversity is a military strength; be a leader in promoting and celebrating diversity. Treat everyone the same. Appreciate people for what they do, not for what they are.

Chapter 58

Touch

We must achieve more than . . .

technology.

—President Lyndon B. Johnson

Technology has introduced the world to fiber optics, but in the process it may have severed the real lines of communication. Too often, ours has become a world of plastic and aluminum gadgets that speak for us and to us in digitalese.

Interestingly, our culture has a hands-off philosophy when— now more than ever—its citizens need a pat on the back. Worse, burning bridges of traditional communications has left us with a wide interpersonal gap. Now, people actually text others from across the same room!

CNN reported that touching actually makes you healthier, both physically and emotionally. It said that activities such as hugging or hand-holding reduces stress, lowers blood pressure, and helps relieve pain. Who could deny that a pat on the back gives you an emotional boost?

Of course, some touching is obviously not appropriate. Regulations regarding sexual harassment include "touching" or "patting" as possible harassment. That can put us in a real quandary. How can we be high-touch in a no-touch society?

Begin by realizing that you can touch others without any physical contact. Some call it the human touch. It's going the extra mile in service to others. For example, you add the human touch when you respond to others with compassion, take an interest in their interests, call them by name, sense their burdens, or help them become what they are capable of becoming.

You can also communicate by something other than email. Pick up the phone—especially if there is any possibility of misunderstanding. Better yet, go sit down and talk in person when there is an opportunity to do so.

What draws you to others in business or social settings can also enhance your leadership in professional settings.

Chapter 59

Giving

You are here to enrich the world,

and you impoverish yourself

if you forget the errand.

—Woodrow Wilson

A tour guide on Michigan's well-known Mackinaw Island was asked about the strangest question he had ever been asked. He replied quickly, "A tourist once asked me if this island was completely surrounded by water."

John Donne's immortal observation that no man is an island has never been truer than it is today. Actually, we are more a peninsula than an island. No matter what our place of service is, we are connected to a much larger community—a community of 7 billion people, to be more specific.

There are many issues that need attention: world hunger, clean water supply, environmental protection, social justice. Globally, there are people who are horribly impoverished, illiterate, underfed, and untreated. Regrettably, many times these issues form the seeds for armed conflict.

The U.S. military is often called on to alleviate suffering through humanitarian missions. We can and should also give back on a personal level.

You've probably heard of the father and son walking along a beach and discovering a starfish. The father picks it up and throws it back in the water. The son reminds him that beaches are filled with starfish and says, "You can't help all of them." Father replied, "No, but I can help that one." The lesson is simple: Our individual efforts can be multiplied by helping, one activity at a time.

You can volunteer for a charitable organization, feed one hungry family near your base, or sponsor the costs of education or food for an international child. Giving back is a great way to help you maintain a healthy balance between personal and professional lives. As President Wilson suggests, the individual who is enriched the most is none other than you.

Chapter 60

Experience

If there is not the war, you don't get

the great general.

—President Theodore Roosevelt

Life is a series of unexpected, and sometimes rough, lessons from that first toddler bump into the coffee table to the last fall out of bed in the nursing home. You couldn't change the first bump, and you probably won't be able to do much about the last fall; but between the episodes, there is a lot to learn about living.

Scientists have recently discovered that there may be 2 billion planets in the galaxy that are suitable for life. The bad news is the nearest one is twelve light-years away, which equals 70 trillion plus miles. So, there probably is no alternative to living and learning right here.

Leaders often get their credentials from Adversity University, where the homework may be painful. But out of the crucible of real-world crisis and hard knocks, experience and savvy are produced that cannot be replicated through textbook learning. Like expensive pottery, value comes from having gone through the fire.

Be thankful for past experiences that were—perhaps, especially—unpleasant. Bumps and bruises can equip you to be a highly professionally, competent, as well as understanding, leader—the kind of leader who prevails against adversaries in uncertain times.

When you hit the next leadership speed bump, realize you are well-equipped by your experience. It will guide you into making winning decisions.

Chapter 61

Example

We're in a fight for our principles, and
our first responsibility is to live
by them.

—President George W. Bush

Military honor guards are ceremonial units that represent the armed forces in such duties as honoring fallen soldiers, guarding national monuments, and escorting the flag at public gatherings. They are volunteers who have been carefully screened for their skill, appearance, attitude, and conduct. They exemplify the best of the best, and they look the part.

Looking good is certainly part of setting the example, but it goes much farther than that. Setting the example is a key leadership trait. Nobel Peace Prize winner Albert Schweitzer went so far as to say, "Example is not the main thing in influencing others. It is the only thing."

As a representative of your nation, your image and your integrity are very important. When someone watches you, he or she is watching both your country and your branch of military service with microscopic vision. You must exemplify the values of your nation and your service—personally and professionally. Think about some ways you can stand out and stand tall.

- Walk your talk. Live your beliefs publicly and privately.
- Speak your mind respectfully. Have the courage to stand against injustice.
- Mind your business. Meet your financial obligations.
- Rely on faith. Strengthen your moral and spiritual beliefs.
- Guard your character. Build invisible fences around thoughts and actions.
- Help others. Be quick to lend a hand.
- Do your duty. Finish your assignments on time.
- Set high standards. Such standards benefit the led as well as the institution.
- Show respect and courtesy to everyone.

Military leaders realize the privilege they have of representing something bigger than themselves. They set the example, both on and off duty.

Chapter 62

Honor

They fought together as brothers-in-arms, they died together, and now they sleep side-by-side. . . . To them, we have a solemn obligation.

—Fleet Admiral of the U.S. Navy Chester Nimitz

Honor has always had a voice. It speaks with hushed gratitude to past warriors and shouts praise to the present.

ABC News reported that thirteen marines were returning from a tour of duty in Afghanistan and made their way to the ticket counter to the cheers of other passengers. The airline customarily upgrades returning military to first-class when seats are available, and only six seats were. When an airline rep announced the marines were on board, seven passengers in first-class volunteered to give up their seats so the soldiers could ride home together.

The gesture was in heartfelt gratitude for the sacrificial service of the marines. Similar deeds happen more frequently than are reported, and rightly so. Giving honor to those who are due honor is an act that always returns more than it surrenders.

You don't have to be on stand-by when it comes to honoring your own. By being proactive in honoring those who serve alongside you, or those who have fallen, you encourage similar honor. How can you show honor?

Say it. Sacrifice should not be met with silence. Be the spokesperson; express public gratitude for behind-the-scenes service.

Demonstrate it; give a material recognition. An inscribed plaque or a decoration or quarterly award could put the finishing touch on a homecoming, a leave, or a completed duty.

Acknowledge it. The recognition others give to you comes with their gratitude. Appreciate it visibly.

Chapter 63

Presence

His cardinal mistake is that

he isolates himself.

—President Abraham Lincoln
on relieving a commanding officer of his duty

I vory towers are unsafe at any height.

The FreeDictionary explains that an ivory tower "is a place or situation that is separated from ordinary life and its problems." It is separated from reality.

You can't book an ivory tower room from an online travel service. You have to construct it yourself and visit it alone. They're built from shoddy materials, such as a false sense of superiority or inferiority, stubbornness, aloofness, or feelings of persecution.

Sometimes ivory towers are camouflaged to look like offices. They become hiding spots as needed. A leader may retreat to his or her tower out of frustration or fear or both. Another excuse for a trip to an ivory tower is elitism or arrogance—to get away from others and their views in order to concentrate on his or her own views.

Leaders should avoid ivory towers for the sake of their leadership and/or their careers. They must get out from behind the desk and circulate among the unit, visiting the troops.

Eyeball-to-eyeball leadership has many advantages. It enables you to explain the whats and whys of the unit mission to the troops. It builds morale. It gives you insights into team strengths or weaknesses, and it gives you a chance to check their capabilities and production. It gives you an opportunity to share personal milestones.

President Reagan once gave a challenge at the Brandenburg Gate in West Berlin, "Tear down this wall!" That's good leadership advice as well.

Chapter 64

Healing

Let us strive on to finish the work
we are in, to bind up the nation's
wounds, to care for him who shall
have borne the battle and for his
widow and his orphan.

—President Abraham Lincoln

War is a horrible reality. Its path of destruction cannot be measured in width or length, and its depth is infinite.

Military chaplains stand alongside hospital beds and flag-draped caskets and grieve war's casualties. They know that some wounds may never heal and grief may be forever borne. Yet they strive on, administering inward the tools of healing to the wounded survivors.

Healing is an intellectual decision. You determine to go on, no matter the cost. The cost may be sizable and may include physical and emotional pain, adjusting to grueling therapeutic regimens and new limitations, and often facing the misunderstandings of the public.

Healing is an emotional decision. You react to the encouragement of others with inner determination. You draw strength from well-wishers and medical staff. You feel the love of friends and family and love them in return.

Healing is a spiritual decision. You decide to draw from your faith. You meditate and pray and read inspirational writings. You let a song from the past lift your spirits and count blessings instead of losses.

Healing is a social decision. You turn wounds and sorrows into causes that will help others cope with their own casualties. In being healed, you become a healer, the greatest healing of all.

Chapter 65

Ego

A man's judgment is best when he
can forget himself and any reputation
he may have acquired and can
concentrate wholly on making
the right decisions.

—Admiral Raymond A. Spruance

Ego is a good thing when it is driven by actual ability; it motivates people to take the lead in problem solving. It is a bad thing when it motivates those same people to think they have the only solution to the problem.

The story is told of a visitor to an air force base who despised maps and backseat driving. Taking a wrong turn at the gate, in spite of his passenger's advice, he was suddenly in a convoy with two other vehicles that had flashing lights and sirens blaring. After he stopped, an officer approached him and said, "Follow us, Sir." When the know-it-all driver asked why, the officer replied, "Because you're on the runway, and that big ol' cargo plane over yonder would like to take off!"

Military leaders are able to set aside egotism, as well as fear of criticism or consequences, in making their decisions. They focus on their organization achieving success, not on personal reward or reputation. They are collaborative—seeking solutions that involve others rather than being Lone Rangers. They avoid turf battles. They don't talk smack. They seek out alternative perspectives. They welcome constructive criticism. They run all options through the filter of team and mission accomplishment.

As General Bruce Clarke said, "Rank is given you to enable you to better serve those above and below you. It is not given for you to practice your idiosyncrasies." View increased rank as the privilege it is; use it wisely and without pretention.

Chapter 66

Ideals

We need to learn to set our course

by the stars, not by the lights

of every passing ship.

—General Omar N. Bradley

The dictionary says that an ideal is a fixed standard, a proven and honorable principle. Idea is a spur of the moment thought or conception, a product of mental activity.

If you are a customer at one of those "As Seen on TV" stores, you'll notice the constant change of products on the shelves. Buy your salad choppers or fake parrots today; they may be gone tomorrow, stacked in a warehouse and marked, "Seemed like a good idea at the time."

Ideals are ideas that have matured and have been accepted through trial and error. Which of the two would seem to be a more accurate navigational point?

Throughout your career, you will be called on to make difficult decisions, sometimes all-important win/lose, life/death decisions. Military leaders maintain their focus on core values and high ideals, not on passing fancy or the latest management fad. Among other benefits, this enables the leader to establish the most vital objectives and priorities.

Some questions you may ask:

- Is this an urgent or important issue?
- Is this decision good for the mission?
- Do I have sufficient resources, personnel, and otherwise, to support the decision?
- Have I considered possible alternative courses of action?
- How will I feel about this decision later on?
- Is this decision consistent with personal and service core values?
- What is the optic of this decision? In other words, how will others perceive it?

Chart your course based on high ideals. Decide for the best and expect best results.

Chapter 67

Creativity

To be successful, you need to be a

person who makes things happen.

—Astronaut James A. Lovell

Some people seem to know how to grow something from nothing, and others know how to grow nothing from something. There seems to be something of a creativity gap.

Leaders who grow organizations live on the edge, renovate traditions, and have a give-it-a-try mentality. They are innovative, naturally curious, and embrace change.

Make sure you add creativity to your leadership model. Contrary to popular rumor, creativity is highly valued in the military. As just one example, consider the individuals who crafted the plan to fly B-25s off the aircraft carrier Hornet to bomb Tokyo in World War II. They were obviously not inside-the-box thinkers.

So how can you be more creative?

First, be an observer. Creativity is all around you. Watch those who are pacesetters and notice what makes them that way. Read the biographies of creative people and learn from them.

Second, challenge your team to be creative and try something new. You could start by asking them to bring you one new idea or method every couple of weeks. Will you get some real duds? Sure, but that is part of the fun of it. You'll be pleasantly surprised at how quickly they, and you, get in the creativity groove and some of the ideas they produce. As author John Steinbeck said, "Ideas are like rabbits. You get a couple and learn how to handle them, and pretty soon you have a dozen."

Take inventory of your creativity skills. There is something in you capable of making a life-changing difference out there.

Chapter 68

Attitude

Optimism is axiomatic with leadership.

—General George Kenney

Your outlook will affect your output.

High achievers are generally very optimistic. They believe in themselves, in their plan, and in the people around them. Their attitude is contagious, making believers out of the doubters and giving greater courage to the stronger.

Attitude makes the difference in the military as well. Military leaders believe in themselves and in their troops. They operate from a position of strength rather than weakness. They are cooperative. They are energetic. They see open windows where there are closed doors. They march with courage to fields of battle.

When you expect the best, you experience the best, even in worst-case situations. The win/win on your countenance comes from the attitude of your mind. You see it there before it becomes a reality.

When you expect the best, others will too. Optimism is caught more often than it is taught. People are more apt to follow someone who believes that something good is going to happen.

You are unlikely to reach your future potential without a positive attitude. Optimism is vital for achievement and courage. Optimistic leaders are open and fair and believe others will reciprocate.

Have a great attitude—be an optimistic leader.

Chapter 69

Adversity

The real leader displays his quality

in his triumphs over adversity,

however great it may be.

—General George Marshall

My mission is to carry on, to make people laugh." Those were the words of Bobby Henline, a veteran of the Iraq war who was burned over 40 percent of his body, lost one ear and part of another, and one hand in an IED explosion. In rehab, Bobby told jokes to other wounded soldiers to help keep their spirits up. At the encouragement of his rehab counselors, he became a stand-up comedian.

TIME.com featured his story in a video. In it, Bobby is seen performing, but also visiting families who lost loved ones in the war. Visiting a twelve-year-old burn victim who was facing his thirtieth reconstructive surgery, he explained later, "I wanted to show him that life can go on."

Thousands of brave men and women have been forever impacted by enemy fire. Some of their wounds are visible; others aren't. But all result in physical, emotional, financial, and relational adjustments. Adversity within the military comes in nonphysical forms as well. It may be a disappointing assignment or performance report.

Without trying to oversimplify a very complicated problem, overcoming adversity has some basic principles.

The first is the decision to adjust to your present condition. With every ounce of spiritual strength, decide to carry on.

The second is to abandon the thought that you're so tough you don't need anyone else. If you have a physical or emotional challenge, don't hesitate to seek professional help. Both military and civilian agencies have innumerable resources available. If you are facing a career disappointment or setback, talk the situation out with a trusted adviser or confidant.

Third, refocus your attention and perspective. Help yourself by helping others. View a setback as a temporary defeat.

You can triumph over adversity, however great it may be.

Chapter 70

Worry

Worry is a word that I don't allow

myself to use.

—General of the U.S. Army Dwight D. Eisenhower

Worry is a costly down payment on a cheap possibility.

Legitimate concern is appropriate. Worry is unproductive and produces inaction. It reduces courage to fear and vision to short-sightedness. It is a negative force in a world of possibilities that has kept untold numbers of people from achieving what they know, deep inside, they can accomplish.

You can't prevent bad things from happening to your good intentions, but you can refuse to let their possibilities become a weight on your shoulders. Worry doesn't have a life of its own; you have to birth it and nurture it. It then becomes your frenemy for life—if you allow it.

Worry always prompts the what-if questions. This throws you off-center and causes you to lose focus. You begin to look for solutions to problems that haven't seen the light of day and will likely never happen. And once you begin asking the endless what-if questions, your next thoughts may start with, I can't, because . . .

Once you have determined a right direction, stay the course. It doesn't hurt to have a backup plan, but don't reach for it too soon. Give your original plan a chance to develop. Think positively and act courageously. Fear doesn't need to be a barrier in your path to success.

Military leaders focus on executing their mission without spending valuable hours worrying about every possible obstacle to its completion. If you've planned the best, delegated the best, and mobilized the best resources, expect the best result.

Chapter 71

Humor

It was involuntary.

They sunk my boat.

—President John F. Kennedy,
answering a question on how he became a war hero

Military leaders need to be serious about humor.

President Kennedy's humorous ad-lib reference to the sinking of the PT-109 boat under his command as a U.S Navy LTJG covered an incident that was actually quite serious. On August 1, 1943, a Japanese destroyer struck Patrol Torpedo Boat 109 (PT-109), shattering Kennedy's vessel and setting it afire. Immediately after the collision, Kennedy helped two crew members make it to safety on the still floating forward hull. He then led his crew on a swim to an island three and a half miles away, while towing an injured sailor. He eventually led his crew to rescue and safety.

JFK was known for his wit almost as much as he was for his wisdom. It was a mark of his military leadership that carried into his presidency.

A leader without a sense of humor is not a pleasant thing. Ultra-seriousness is often judgmental and critical of others. It also is seen as a weakness of character, springing from feelings of inferiority.

A day without at least one funny incident isn't a normal day. A trip to the mall is example enough. The sights and sounds of people being people will always have a measure of hilarity. And that is certainly true in the military as well. Just look around. Take time to laugh — including laughing at yourself. It's time well-spent and a natural stress reliever. It's a valuable coping mechanism for dealing with a tumultuous world.

Laughter also provides an instant connection with those whom you lead. It will help your team overcome the significant challenges and difficulties of military life. The military is serious business, but there is a time and place to have fun. Humor is not a sign of weakness; it is a sign of human strength and a valuable leadership trait.

About the Authors

Stan Toler is a leader, teacher, and best-selling author of nearly 100 books. He served as vice president for John C. Maxwell's INJOY Leadership Institute for more than a decade, teaching seminars and training church and organization leaders and major corporation leaders, nationally and internationally. Over one million people have attended his seminars.

Robert Redwine is a retired Brigadier General. He served a total of nearly 28 years in the Air Force and Air Force Reserve in the intelligence and missile operations career fields, including deployment as the acting USCENTAF Director of Intelligence for Operations Iraqi Freedom and Enduring Freedom. General Redwine is a member of the American Legion. He currently works as an attorney and as an adjunct professor teaching American federal government.